how to speak
emoji
love

Anna Mrowiec

EBURY
PRESS

1 3 5 7 9 10 8 6 4 2

Ebury Press, an imprint of Ebury Publishing
20 Vauxhall Bridge Road
London SW1V 2SA

Ebury Press is part of the Penguin Random House group of companies
whose addresses can be found at global.penguinrandomhouse.com

Copyright © Ebury Press 2016

Author: Anna Mrowiec

First published by Ebury Press in 2016
www.eburypublishing.co.uk

A CIP catalogue record for this book is available from the British Library

ISBN 9781785033414

Printed and bound: TBB, a.s. Slovakia

Designed by seagulls.net

contents

basic language tips

There are a handful of ways to think about emoji translation. Here's a couple of the techniques I used to make this book:

- Literal translation: Sometimes you find the exact emoji you need, for example, 👽 for the movie *Alien,* and at other times you need a handful.

- Rebus: When an emoji is used to replace a word or part of a word. For example, 🔍 + 📅 = Friday.

- Visual pun: Using emoji to imply a different meaning than originally intended. For example, 🍆 for… well, you can guess.

- Telling the story: sometimes you can take it a bit further, and play out your intended meaning. So for 'break the ice', you could have emojis act it out: 🏂 🔨 🧊

To make your own emoji translation, get creative! Don't worry about verbs or abstract concepts, focus on clever pairings, be literal when you can (e.g. 'shooting pain' uses 🔫 for 'shooting'), and don't be afraid to use the emoji with words in them (e.g. 🔜). Finally, have fun and don't take it too seriously; chances are people will understand the general gist of what you're trying to say and you'll get points for being creative regardless.

Emoji Dictionary

The easiest and most effective way of showing how completely you love someone. All you see is love.

The kissy face – an upgrade on the more restrained 'x'.

'My angel!' A lovely term of endearment.

For when you're feeling a bit cheeky, or when you want to subtly suggest something to do with tongues.

For when subtle simply won't cut the mustard.

Because cats can feel love too! The vast array of cat-face emojis keep friends of felines very happy.

'Baby', a term of endearment that never seems to go out of fashion. Or you can use it to apply gentle pressure if feeling broody.

Just a girl, standing next to a boy, asking him to love her.

  Or the same-sex equivalent.

 The bunny girls are usually used to signify friendship (or a girls' night out). But they can also be helpful in relationships if your partner is also your BFF.

 For when you're in need of a bit of attention.

 If you really, truly love someone, a big pink heart will hover in the air between you.

 Often used wistfully when not with your loved one, it's a fantastic statement of intent for when you're next together.

 For when things are good. If you're not using this one a lot with your sweetheart, perhaps you should reconsider things…

Kisses!

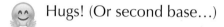 Another way of symbolising a kiss. But the saucy, slightly open mouth can also be highly suggestive.

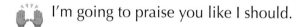 Hugs! (Or second base…)

I'm going to praise you like I should.

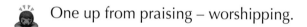 One up from praising – worshipping.

Begging is not very dignified but sometimes a necessity. Particularly if you've done something wrong.

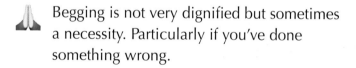 Also helpful if you're apologising, although if you've cheated this is one of the very few times an emoji might not cut it. Interflora's number is 08444535600.

For use when your lover is being unreasonable, or 'crabby'. Or to represent an STD.

 If I have to explain this emoji, then this book might not be the one for you. It's as phallic as they come.

 A close second.

 At a push.

 Really scraping the barrel.

 For when you need to 'pop' one.

 Another pretty obvious one. Peachy!

 My milkshake brings all the boys to the yard.

If you like a stereotype, this is the way to a woman's heart.

A nice way of suggesting a first date, if you follow with a **?**

The different clocks on offer will help to arrange an exact time. This is an ideal one for a date.

Another way of suggesting a 'date'.

A nice accompaniment for said date.

A fancy date!

A really rubbish date.

Breakfast? Best used if sent before an evening date.

You should always shower your loved one with these.

 Again, an emoji doesn't always cut it here, but it's a good way to show your intentions are honourable.

 Bigger. And therefore better.

 Quite self-explanatory, but look at all the great colours it comes in! 💚💙🤍💙

 Love grows year on year.

 Shot through the heart, and you're to blame.

 I hope you never have to use this one.

 Because if you're not with them, you should always be running to your love.

They're the best!

 Your special day is finally here!

 The closest you'll get to signifying 'groom'.

 Lots of different religious locations for your wedding! (Courtesy of the latest iOS update).

 Not a 'love hospital' but a 'love hotel', popular in Japan where they can be rented by the hour. You can use this emoji to suggest a saucy rendez-vous.

 Only use this with permission or you'll find yourself in a world of trouble.

 In the olden days, before emoji, lovers used to use these to talk to each other.

🔓 There's a nice alternative meaning for the lock and key… 😉

🛏 The bed – represents either nap time or kinky time.

🚺 The more traditional toilet symbol, and good for suggesting a quickie when in a bar.

🔞 If this is a strict rule for you, this important emoji will be useful in ascertaining the truth. You could even ask for some 🆔.

🔜 If you're not ready to commit, keep your lover at bay with this and other empty promises.

👴 I want to grow old with you.

👵 And I, you.

Pick-Up Lines

Yo, baby.

Hi honey!

You're a bombshell!

Sexy beast…

Silver fox.

You are smoking hot, sweetheart!

Is this your lucky night?

How big is it?

You've got a great pair.

Do you believe in love at first sight, or should I walk by again?

I bet you're an animal in the sack…

Are you a racehorse? Because you've been running round my head all night.

What a cattle market…

I'm having a whale of a time!

I'm writing a phonebook? Can I have your number?

Do you live in a cornfield? Because I'm stalking you.

Did you have lucky charms for breakfast? Because you look magically delicious!

Is your dad a drug dealer? Because you're so dope!

Is your dad a thief? Because he stole the stars and put them in your eyes.

I must be a snowflake, because I've fallen for you.

Was your dad a baker? Because you've got a nice set of buns.

All I want for Christmas is you.

I love animals.

Does your left eye hurt? Because you've been looking right all day.

I was feeling off, but you turned me on.

I'll cook you dinner if you cook me breakfast.

I don't have a library card, but do you mind if I check you out?

How old are you?

Wink wink.

Wanna join the mile high club?

Let me teach you about the birds and the bees.

Nice jeans! Can I get in them?

Someone needs to call the police, because you're da bomb.

You're one hot babe!

Dating Tips

Smell good.

Don't text back straightaway.

Don't eat spaghetti.

Don't be an open book.

Never date a married man.

On the first date, only engage in light petting.

Not sex.

Don't chew with your mouth open.

Say it, don't spray it.

Keep it in your trousers.

Don't mention the future.

Don't be too cheesy.

Act like you're busy and successful.

  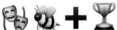

Don't take any shit.

Stay emotionally cool.

Don't hog the food.

Make sure your gaydar is working.

Give them a present to break the ice.

Don't get too drunk.

Chivalry isn't dead.

Don't be bullish.

Make eye contact.

Don't break wind.

The whole evening shouldn't be spent in the bathroom.

Beauty is in the eye of the beholder.

Actions speak louder than words.

Don't count your chickens before they hatch.

Don't be cheeky.

It takes two to tango.

The journey of a thousand miles begins with one step.

30

Things Not to Say on a First Date

You look nervous.

Cat got your tongue?

My ex-girlfriend loved cats.

I think I'm in love…

Is your friend single?

Isn't this actually kind of our third date?

You're going out of town for six months??

I forgot my purse.

Is that a gun or… ? Oh.

I sure hope you shaved.

I thought you were gay…

I was just dreaming about our future children.

You'd get on so well with my wife.

Do you want to go to a strip bar?

I don't have any hobbies.

Can I read your diary?

I got to level 100 in World of Warcraft!

I only like Candy Crush Saga.

You could lose a few pounds.

This is my second date today!

I'm a real ladies man.

You're a bit younger than me...

I have to attend a sexual harassment sensitivity training workshop...

You can pay.

You've charmed the pants right off me.

Beggars can't be choosers.

I'm on a liquid diet.

Can you make it as spicy as possible?

Can we be friends with benefits?

I have many sexually transmitted diseases.

Let's get freaky!

Don't call me, I'll call you.

Sorry, I'm engaged.

Breaking Up

We need to talk.

I'm moving to Yemen.

This is the end.

END

You're not Mr Right.

I need to find myself.

I need an older woman.

I've given up on men.

I've been seeing people behind your back.

Talk to the hand…

It's not the right time.

I'm moving out.

My cat doesn't like you.

I need to spend more time at work.

You're a pain in the ass.

We're moving too fast.

42

You're too immature.

You're sh*t.

I want to DIE!

You looked better last night.

I'm taking the dog.

Grow some balls!

Suck it up!

You bore me to tears…

You're a pillock.

Go f*ck yourself!

Cry me a river…

Don't call me, I'll call you.

Do I have to paint you a picture?

I've got to shoot off.

In the
Bedroom

You turn me on.

   ON!

Wanna bang?

 ?

Wanna hump?

 ?

Wanna screw?

 ?

Might not be the best idea…

47

Bedroom eyes…

I've got the horn.

Wow!

Missionary.

I've got something special in mind.

Cowgirl.

Reverse cowgirl.

Doggy.

Banana split.

Scissoring.

The golden shower.

Threesome.

Dogging.

Spanking.

Ways to Say
I Love You

I love ewe.

From the bottom of my heart.

I'm bananas for you!

You're my boo.

I'm sweet on you.

I love that we share all the same interests!

Don't break my heart.

You drive me crazy.

I'm burning for you.

You're the world to me.

I'm a smitten kitten.

You put a spell on me.

You make me feel young again!

I worship you!

You're my sunshine!

I'm hooked on you!

You're the girl of my dreams!

I'm strong when I'm on your shoulders.

You take my breath away.

You're the world's best boyfriend.

God sent an angel.

I'm head over heels.

I love you to the moon and back.

Meeting the Parents

I would like you to meet my parents.

Like a lamb to the slaughter.

Can I see all the baby photos?

No, I'm not planning to become a housewife…

You and your mother are like twins!

So are you guys loaded or what?

Yeah I love prescription pills!

We've got some news…

Just joking!

I spend most of my days gaming…

Dinner looks OK, but I might order a pizza…

Does the dog like vodka?

In two months I'm not her teacher anymore…

Your fish would make great sushi!

Living Together

Living in sin.

We should just put your stuff in storage…

I think I'm allergic to your cat.

It's cheaper to live in the suburbs.

We've only got one toilet.

You need to go out. My friends are coming for girls' night.

Did you hear that??

We're out of toilet paper…

Let's stop fighting.

I'm sorry.

Have you done the meter readings?

Stop making a mess!

Don't try to change me.

No phones at dinner!

It's poker night! No girls allowed.

You left ALL the lights on!

Can you play music loudly so I can go to the toilet?

Can you choose something to watch on Netflix already?

The Proposal

It's time.

A dozen red roses.

The best things come in small packages.

You light up my world.

My dog ate the ring!

Please make me the luckiest man in the world!

Can I have a bigger diamond?

I want to grow old with you.

I would die for you.

We're soulmates.

You're the one!

We were made for each other.

I'll never look at another woman again.

It's been a real emotional rollercoaster.

I'll call my parents with the good news.

The Wedding

She said yes!

I had to kiss a lot of frogs to find my prince.

Hen party!

Church bells.

I've booked the marquee!

Ring bearer.

Page boy.

Flower girls.

Vicar.

Rabbi.

Morning suits or tuxedos?

Wedding tax.

  + + +

Gift list.

No red wine.

White food only.

      ✓

   ✗

For better, for worse.

For richer, for poorer.

In sickness and in health.

To honour and obey.

Till death us do part.

Grandad's drunk!

You can't have your cake and eat it too.

Don't swim in the fountain.

Dancing till two.

Raising Children

Baby shower.

Goodbye sleep!

Teething.

Booties.

Pacifier.

We're coping just fine.

My baby is allergic to dairy.

Can you carry a baby in a handbag?

Nappy.

Like taking candy from a baby.

My child is bilingual!

Potty training.

His first word was 'Olaf'.

Peekaboo!

Baby talk.

Don't throw the baby out with the bath water.

Tooth fairy.

No sugar before bedtime.

Don't cry over spilt milk.

Love Songs

'Baby' JUSTIN BIEBER FT. LUDACRIS

'Drunk in Love' BEYONCÉ FT. JAY-Z

'River Deep – Mountain High' IKE & TINA TURNER

'Wild Thing' THE TROGGS

'Eternal Flame' THE BANGLES

'Hello' LIONEL RICHIE

'Cheek to Cheek' FRED ASTAIRE

'Signed, Sealed, Delivered, I'm Yours' STEVIE WONDER

'The Way You Look Tonight' FRANK SINATRA

'The Power of Love' FRANKIE GOES TO HOLLYWOOD

'I Say a Little Prayer' ARETHA FRANKLIN

'XO' BEYONCÉ

'Story of My Life' ONE DIRECTION

'Angel' SHAGGY FT. RAYVON

'Angels' ROBBIE WILLIAMS

'Chasing Cars' SNOW PATROL

'Let's Get It on' MARVIN GAYE

'Three Times a Lady' LIONEL RICHIE

'Love Story' TAYLOR SWIFT

'Runaway' THE CORRS

'Let Her Go' PASSENGER

'Don't Stop Believin'' JOURNEY

'The First Time Ever I Saw Your Face' ROBERTA FLACK

'Baby Love' THE SUPREMES

'Fallin'' ALICIA KEYS

'Lovefool' THE CARDIGANS

'Wild Horses' THE ROLLING STONES

'Back for Good' TAKE THAT

'Bleeding Love' LEONA LEWIS

'Strangers in the Night' FRANK SINATRA

'The Love Cats' THE CURE

'I Just Called to Say I Love You' STEVIE WONDER

'What a Diff'rence a Day Makes!' DINAH WASHINGTON

'I Wanna Dance with Somebody' WHITNEY HOUSTON

'Here, There and Everywhere' THE BEATLES

'Crazy in Love' BEYONCÉ FT. JAY-Z

'We Found Love in a Hopeless Place'
RIHANNA FT. CALVIN HARRIS

'Two in a Million' S CLUB 7

'Kiss from a Rose' SEAL

'Thank You For Loving Me' BON JOVI

89

'Tonight, I Celebrate My Love'

PEABO BRYSON AND ROBERTA FLACK

'The Wind Beneath My Wings' BETTE MIDLER

'My Heart Will Go On' CELINE DION

'Can't Smile Without You' BARRY MANILOW

'Time After Time' CYNDI LAUPER

'Is This Love' BOB MARLEY & THE WAILERS

'Unchained Melody' THE RIGHTEOUS BROTHERS

'Love to Love You Baby' DONNA SUMMER

'Girl' THE BEATLES

'Woman' JOHN LENNON

'Un-break My Heart' TONI BRAXTON

'I Melt with You' MODERN ENGLISH

'I'm Gonna Be (500 Miles)' THE PROCLAIMERS

Romantic Movies

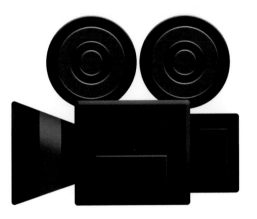

Magic Mike

The Notebook

Casablanca

Titanic

Dirty Dancing

Knocked Up

The Princess Bride

Brokeback Mountain

Gone with the Wind

Breakfast at Tiffany's

Ghost

(500) Days of Summer

Four weddings and a funeral

You've Got Mail

Beauty and the Beast

The Sound of Music

King Kong

Singin' in the Rain

The Graduate

An Officer and a Gentleman

Water for Elephants

The Time Traveler's Wife

The Bodyguard

Up

Manhattan

How to Lose a Guy in 10 Days

The Holiday

Walk the Line

His Girl Friday

Twilight

Friends with Benefits

Sex and the City

Sex and the City 2

27 Dresses

Crazy, Stupid, Love

She's the Man

Cinderella

Blue Valentine

The Princess Diaries

Far From the Madding Crowd

The Princess and the Frog

My Best Friend's Wedding

Les Misérables

Paper Towns

Top Gun

Pitch Perfect

American Beauty

Cold Mountain

One Day

Moulin Rouge

The Little Mermaid

Chocolat

The Proposal

The Wedding Singer

Sleeping Beauty

Fifty Shades of Grey

Quotes About Love

'You are my sun, my moon and all my stars'.

E. E. CUMMINGS

'Come live with me and be my love'.

CHRISTOPHER MARLOWE

'Let me not to the marriage of true minds/
Admit impediments'. WILLIAM SHAKESPEARE

'I never saw so sweet a face'. JOHN CLARE

'Love actually is all around.' LOVE ACTUALLY

'She walks in beauty, like the night'.
LORD BYRON

'Love is composed of a single soul inhabiting two bodies.' ARISTOTLE

'Oh, may your silhouette never dissolve on the beach'. PABLO NERUDA

'Absence makes the heart grow fonder.' UNKNOWN

'Oh, my Luve's like a red, red rose'. ROBERT BURNS

'He was my North, my South, my East and West'.

W.H. AUDEN

'Shall I compare thee to a summer's day?'

WILLIAM SHAKESPEARE

'I love thee to the depth and breadth and height my soul can reach.' ELIZABETH BARRETT BROWNING

'I'm walking on sunshine'. KATRINA AND THE WAVES

'All's fair in love and war.' FRANK SMEDLEY

'When love is not madness, it is not love.'
PEDRO CALDERÓN DE LA BARCA

'Nobody puts Baby in a corner.' DIRTY DANCING

'Two lovers in the rain have no need of an umbrella.'
JAPANESE PROVERB

'Soul meets soul on lovers' lips'. PERCY BYSSHE SHELLEY

'Love is the greatest refreshment.' PABLO PICASSO

'Love cannot be cured by herbs'. OVID

'Come on baby, light my fire'. THE DOORS

'Love doesn't make the world go round. Love is
what makes the ride worthwhile.' FRANKLIN P. JONES

'Love is a game that two can play and both win.'
EVA GABOR

'Two souls, one heart.' FRENCH SAYING USED ON POESY RINGS

'Stolen kisses are always sweetest.' LEIGH HUNT

'If your heart is a volcano, how shall you expect flowers to bloom?' KHALIL GIBRAN

'Love is a battlefield'. PAT BENATAR